Contents

Stories with familiar settings

From 'Percy and the Rabbit' by Nick Butterworth

Percy the Park Keeper was in the park.
A rabbit came to see him.
Percy said, "Look at the snow."

The rabbit said, "Look at the mice. They're playing
in my house."
Percy said, "Mice! Please don't
play in the rabbit's house."
The mice went away.

Get started

Look at the story. Find the missing words.

1. Percy the Park Keeper was in
the _____.

2. A _____ came to
see him.

3. Percy said, "Look at the
_____."

4. The rabbit said, "Look at the _____.

5. They're playing in my _____."

Try these

Add your own words to each sentence.

1. The rabbit is _____.

2. Percy is _____.

3. The mice are _____.

4. The park is _____.

5. The rabbit's house is _____.

Now try these

1. What do you think the park looks like? Draw a picture of the park.

2. What do you think the rabbit's house looks like? Draw a picture of the mice playing in the rabbit's house.

3. What are the mice saying? Add speech bubbles to your pictures and write what the mice are saying.

Fairy Stories

From **'Rumpelstiltskin'** by
Anne Walter

Once upon a time, a poor, foolish miller
lived with his daughter.

The miller wanted to please the king. So, one day,
he took his daughter to the king's palace.

"My girl can spin straw into gold," the
miller lied, boastfully. The king was pleased.
He loved gold.

Get started

Look at the story. Find the missing words.

Once _____ a time a poor,
_____ miller lived with his
_____. The miller _____ to
please the king. So, one day, he took his
daughter to the _____ palace.

Try these

Add your own words to each sentence.

1. The miller was a _____ man.

2. The king was a _____ man.

3. The daughter was a _____ girl.

4. The palace was very _____.

5. The straw was _____.

Now try these

1. Draw a picture of the miller at his house.

2. Draw a picture of the king at the palace.

3. What are they saying? Add speech bubbles to your pictures and write what each character says.

4. Write a sentence about the miller telling the king a lie.

Fantasy Stories

From **'Arthur's Fantastic Party'** by Joseph Theobald

One day, Arthur had an idea.
He said, "I'll have a party for all the best, most fantastic animals!"
Flora said, "That's a good idea.
I'll tell everyone."
Flora told the three pigs …
… who told the wolf …
… who told the bears.
Soon all the animals were talking about Arthur's fantastic party.

Get started

Arthur is planning a party for all the best, most fantastic animals. Draw and label pictures of the party guests.

1. Draw and label a picture of Arthur.

2. Draw and label a picture of Flora.

3. Draw and label a picture of the three pigs.

4. Draw and label a picture of the wolf.

5. Draw and label a picture of the bears.

Try these

Add your own words.

1. Arthur said, "_____."

2. Flora said, "_____."

3. The three pigs said,
"_____."

4. The wolf said, "_____."

5. The bears said, "_____."

Now try these

1. Who else will come to Arthur's party? Make up your own fantastic animal party guest. Draw a picture.

2. What will your animal say? Draw a speech bubble and write what they say.

3. Make an invitation for the party.

4. Write a sentence about the party games Arthur wants to play.

Poetry: The Senses

'Night Sounds' by Berlie Doherty

When I lie in bed
I think I can hear
The stars being switched on
I think I can.

And I think I can hear
The moon
Breathing.

But I have to be still.
So still.
All the house is sleeping.
Except for me.

Then I think I can hear it.

Get started

In this poem are some sounds that can be heard at night.
Write a sound for each of these night-time things.

1. An owl

2. A clock

3. A fox

4. A mouse

5. A bat

Try these

Use your ideas to finish these sentences.

1. When I lie in ...

2. I can hear ...

3. I can see ...

4. I can smell ...

5. I feel ...

Now try these

1. Draw a picture of you lying in bed.

2. Draw a picture of your garden at night.

3. Label your picture with all the different noises in the garden at night. Add to your picture if you want to.

4. Write a sentence about noises you can hear at night.

Poetry: Patterns

**'Some Things Don't Make Any Sense
At All' by Judith Vorst**

My mom says I'm her sugarplum.
My mom says I'm her lamb.
My mom says I'm completely perfect
Just the way I am.
My mom says I'm a super-special wonderful
terrific little guy.
My mom just had another baby.
Why?

Get started

What does your family say about you ...

1. when you are naughty?

2. when you are kind?

3. when you are hungry?

4. when you are sleepy?

5. when you are fed up?

Try these

Use your ideas to finish these sentences.

1. My mum says I'm …

2. My mum says my sister or brother is …

3. My Grandad says I'm …

4. My friend says I'm …

5. I think they are all …

Now try these

1. Draw a picture of the boy in the poem with his pregnant mom.

2. What are they saying to each other? Add speech bubbles to your pictures and write what each character says.

3. Draw a picture of you with someone you care about.

4. What are you saying to each other? Add speech bubbles to your pictures and write what each character says.

5. Write a sentence to the boy in the poem to tell him his mum will still love him even when she has a new baby.

Poetry: My Favourite

'Things I Like In The Sea That Go By Swimmingly' by Grace Nichols

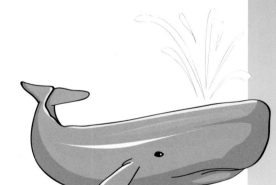

Jellyfish
Starfish
Flying fish
Seals

Dolphins
Octopuses
Otters
Eels

Crabs
Turtles
Weevers
Manatees

Sea lions
Walruses
Shrimps
Whales

But best of all
I like Mermaids

Get started

Find these things in the poem.

1. One thing beginning with C

2. Two things beginning with O

3. Three things beginning with W

4. Four things beginning with S

Try these

Write a sentence to describe each of these creatures.

1. A starfish

2. A dolphin

3. A jellyfish

4. A turtle

Now try these

1. The poem is a list. Write a list of other things that can be found in the sea.

2. Draw an underwater picture including six sea creatures from the poem.

3. Draw speech bubbles and write what the creatures in your picture are saying.

Writing Instructions

Can you make a hard, small thing turn into a tall, green thing?

Yes, you can. You can grow a beanstalk. This is how!

What you need: a stone, soil, a bean seed, a pot.

Get a pot with a hole in the base.
Put a stone in the pot.
Put some soil in the pot.
Place the bean seed in the pot.
Add some soil on top.
Pat it down so the top is flat.

Get started

For each item, write 'yes' if you need it to grow a beanstalk and 'no' if you don't.

1. a pot

2. a flower

3. a stone

4. some pegs

5. some soil

Try these

Read the instructions again. Find the missing bossy verb (imperative).

1. _____ a pot with a hole in the base.

2. _____ a stone in the pot.

3. _____ the bean seed in the pot.

4. _____ some soil on top.

5. _____ it down so the top is flat.

Now try these

1. Write an instruction to tell people to water the seed.

2. Draw and label a picture that shows how to play a game of catch.

3. Write a set of instructions to tell people how to butter some bread.

4. Write four instructions that would help a new child in your class know what to do in the mornings when they get to school.

Writing Simple Reports

Robin

The robin has a bright red face and breast, just like on a Christmas card. It looks fatter in winter, when it fluffs itself up to keep warm.

A male sings his lovely song all year round – sometimes even at night. He's a fierce fighter, too.

Get started

Find the missing words.

1. The robin has a bright _____ face and breast.

2. It looks _____ in winter.

3. It fluffs itself up to keep

_____.

4. A male sings his _____ song all year round.

5. He's a _____ fighter, too.

Try these

Add your own words.

1. The robin has _____ wings.

2. It has _____ legs.

3. It has a _____ beak.

4. It likes to eat _____ worms.

5. It has _____ eyes.

Now try these

1. Draw and label a picture of a robin.

2. Find out a new fact about robins.

3. Write a sentence about a different type of bird.

4. Write a sentence about birds in winter.

Writing Simple Recounts

I am a chick

I hatched out of an egg that my mother laid.

I pecked my way out of the shell with my beak.

It was very hard work.

Get started

Add your own words.

1. The chick _____ with its claws.

2. The chick _____ its little wings.

3. The chick _____ in the dirt.

4. The chick _____ at the corn.

5. The chick _____ in the hay.

Try these

Write one thing that you did ...

1. this morning.

2. yesterday.

3. last week.

4. last year.

5. when you were a baby.

Now try these

1. Draw the chick pecking in the farmyard.

2. Draw you as a baby.

3. Draw you on your last birthday.

4. Write a sentence about something your friend did yesterday.